HEAL WIT

N

DR. B'S PHYSIOLOGY OF THE VAGUS NERVE

An Overview of the Cranial Nerves, With a Focus on the Importance of the VAGUS Nerve and Understanding Its Full Healing Potential

Dr. Sasha J. Blaskovich and

Ifiokobong Ene

PHYSIOLOGY OF THE VAGUS NERVE

ISBN: 9798862046243

This edition of HEAL WITH THE VAGUS NERVE - Dr. B's Physiology of the Vagus Nerve by Dr. Sasha J. Blaskovich and Ifiokobong Ene is published by the authors using Kindle Direct Publishing.

Table of Contents

INTRODUCTION....6

CHAPTER 1

INTRODUCING THE NERVOUS SYSTEM....9

CENTRAL NERVOUS SYSTEM....10

The Brain....11

Regions of the Brain....12

The Spinal Cord....14

White and Gray Matter....15

PERIPHERAL NERVOUS SYSTEM....18

Sympathetic and Parasympathetic Nervous System....20

CHAPTER 2

ANATOMY & PHYSIOLOGY OF THE CRANIAL NERVES....21

Olfactory Nerve....22

Optic Nerve....24

Oculomotor Nerve....25

Trochlear Nerve....27

Trigeminal Nerve....28

Abducens Nerve....30

Facial Nerve....31

Vestibulocochlear Nerve....32

Glossopharyngeal Nerve....34

Accessory Nerve....36

Hypoglossal Nerve....37

CHAPTER 3

PHYSIOLOGICAL FUNCTIONS OF THE VAGUS NERVE....38

What's Affected by the Vagus Nerve?....39

CHAPTER 4

THE ROLE OF THE VAGUS NERVE IN INFLAMMATION....42

Overview of Inflammation....42

Acute Inflammation....42

Phases..43
Vascular Phase..44
Cellular Phase..45
Outcome of Acute Inflammation..46
Pus Formation..47
Chronic Inflammation..50
Reducing Inflammation is a Function of the Vagus Nerve...............54
Vagal Tone and its Importance..55
The Brain – Gut Connection..56
The Nervous System and the Vagus Nerve......................................57
Neurotransmitters..58
Vagus Nerve and Better Mental Health: An Interesting Connection...........59
CHAPTER 5
STRESS AND THE NERVOUS SYSTEM......................................61
The Basics of Stress..61
Stress Hormones..62
Types of Stress..65
Acute Stress..65
Episodic Acute Stress..66
Chronic Stress..66
Stress and the Nervous System..67
Effects of Stress on the Brain..68
CHAPTER 6
ACTIVATING THE HEALING POWERS OF THE VAGUS NERVE.........76
The Deep-Breathing Technique..79
Getting Started..80
Loving Kindness Meditation..82
Yoga-like Stretching/Poses..84
Massage..88
Cold Water Exposure..89
Tai Chi..90

Sun Exposure……………………………………………………………**91**

Fasting……………………………………………………………………**91**

Closing Remarks…………………………………………………………**92**
REFERENCES……………………………………………………………**93**

INTRODUCTION

The Vagus nerve is the longest nerve in the autonomic nervous system. It emanates from the brain. Information flowing through the Vagus nerve goes to and from the brain surface to organs and tissues of the body. Vagus is derived from the Latin word "wandering." It is named so because the Vagus nerve wanders from the brain to the organs in the abdomen, chest, and the neck.

Many people are yet to understand that the Vagus nerve is probably the most important nerve in the human body. Compared to others, what happens in the Vagus nerve doesn't stay there. It links the brain stem to the lungs, heart, and the gut. It innervates nearly most of the deep organs within us. It also innervates the liver, the gallbladder, the spleen, female reproductive organs, ureter, tongue, kidney, ears, and the neck.

Dysfunction of the Vagus nerve can trigger a wide range of problems such as bradycardia, obesity, fainting, gastrointestinal disorders, mood disorders, etc.

On the other hand, stimulation of the Vagus nerve improves the following conditions:

- Heart disease
- Anxiety disorder
- Tinnitus

- Migraines
- Leaky gut
- Obesity
- Mood disorders
- Poor blood circulation etc.

HEAL WITH THE VAGUS NERVE - DR. B'S PHYSIOLOGY OF THE VAGUS NERVE explains in simple and easy-to-understand words, the basic physiology of the Vagus nerve and how to access its full healing potentials.

We understand that not everyone who purchases this book is medically-inclined, and so, it is written with no unnecessary medical jargons. It is brief, simple, and "straight to the point."

In this book: "HEAL WITH THE VAGUS NERVE - DR. B'S PHYSIOLOGY OF THE VAGUS NERVE: An Overview of the Cranial Nerves, With a Focus on the Importance of the VAGUS Nerve and Understanding Its Full Healing Potentials", you will discover:

- The basics of the nervous system
- Anatomy & Physiology of the cranial nerves
- Physiological functions of the Vagus nerve
- The role of the Vagus nerve in inflammation
- The brain-gut connection
- Activating the healing powers of the Vagus nerve

Your criticisms and reviews are welcome.

The Publishers:

(drb@drblaskovich.com)

(medicalresearch271@gmail.com)

CHAPTER 1

INTRODUCING THE NERVOUS SYSTEM

The nervous system is one of the most incredible and complex systems in the human body. It is a control system, meaning that it is involved in the control of body functions. There are two major control systems in the body:

- The nervous system
- The endocrine system

The nervous system controls every activity in the human body. It performs its function quicker than the endocrine system. Basically, the nervous system comprises of two sub-types:

- The central nervous system
- The peripheral nervous system

CENTRAL NERVOUS SYSTEM

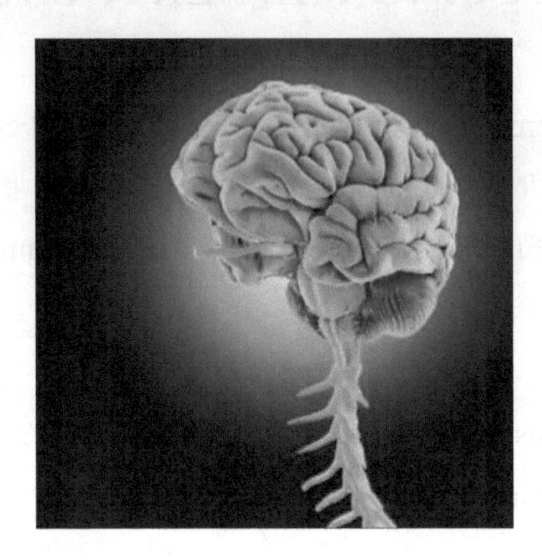

The central nervous system consists of the brain and the spinal cord. The brain is housed within the skull or the cranial cavity. The spinal cord on the other hand travels from the back of the brain, and through the center of the spine, terminating in the lumbar region of the lower back.

Both the brain and the spinal cord are located within the meninges. The meninges are a layer of protective membranes.

A lot of studies have been done on the central nervous system by both anatomists and physiologists, but then, there is still a lot to be learnt, and much more to be understood. The central nervous system holds many secrets; it controls our movements, thoughts, desires, and emotions. It takes charge of our heart rate, breathing, synthesis and release of some hormones, body temperature, etc.

The optic nerve, retina, olfactory epithelium, and olfactory nerves are in some cases, considered to be a part of the central nervous system alongside the spinal cord and the brain. Why is this so? Well, it is because they have a direct link with the brain tissue without the need for intermediate nerve fibers.

Let us study part of the central nervous system in detail.

The Brain

The brain happens to be the most complex organ in the human body. The largest part of the brain (by volume) is the cerebral cortex. It contains about 15-33 billion neurons. Each neuron is connected to thousands of other neurons.

All in all, there are around 100 billion neurons and a thousand billion glial cells in the human brain. Glial cells are "supporting cells." The human brain takes up no less than 20% of our body's total energy.

The brain serves as the body's central control module. It is responsible for the coordination of the body's activities including physical motion, hormone secretion, memory consolidation, and the sensation of emotions.
To perform these functions at optimal capacity, some parts of the brain play very unique roles. However, it is worth noting that most higher functions, such as problem-solving, reasoning, creativity, etc. involve a lot of networking.

Your brain is split roughly into four lobes:

Temporal Lobe: The temporal lobe is concerned with processing sensory input and assigning emotional interpretation. It is also involved in memory consolidation (laying down long-term memories). Language perception is also housed in the temporal lobe.

Occipital Lobe: The occipital lobe houses the visual cortex. It is responsible for visual processing.

Parietal Lobe: This is responsible for integration of sensory information such as spatial awareness, navigation, and touch. The touch sensation is sent to the parietal lobe. It is also involved in language processing.

Frontal Lobe: It lies at the front part of the brain. The frontal lobe contains neurons sensitive to dopamine. It is involved in reward, attention, motivation, short-term memory, and planning.

Regions of the Brain

Let us examine in detail some specific regions of the brain:

Basal Ganglia: it controls voluntary motor movements, decisions about what motor activities to perform, and procedural learning. The basal ganglia are affected by pathological conditions such as Huntington's disease and Parkinson's disease.

Cerebellum: it plays a very important role in precise motor control, attention and language. If your cerebellum is damaged, you will experience ataxia – which is disruption of motor control.

Broca's Area: Broca's area is located on the left side of the brain (and on the right side in some left-handed individuals). The Broca's area is involved in language processing. If the Broca's area is damaged, the affected person will be unable to speak. However, he or she can still understand speech. Stuttering is usually associated with an underactive Broca's area.

Corpus Callosum: The corpus callosum is a band of nerve fibers that connect the right and left hemispheres. The corpus callosum is the largest portion of white matter in the brain. It facilitates communication between the two brain hemispheres. Children suffering from dyslexia have a small-sized corpus callosum. People who are left-handed or ambidextrous typically have large a corpus callosum.

Medulla Oblongata: The medulla oblongata extends below the skull. It is involved in involuntary effects such as breathing, vomiting, sneezing, and blood pressure maintenance.

Hypothalamus: The hypothalamus sits just above the brainstem. It is the size of an almond. The hypothalamus secretes several neurohormones and influences thirst, hunger, and body temperature.

Thalamus: Well-positioned in the center of the brain, thalamus receives motor and sensory input and transmits it to the rest of the cerebral cortex. The thalamus plays an active role in the regulation of sleep, consciousness, alertness, and awareness.

Amygdala: The amygdala lies within the temporal lobe. It is involved in emotional responses (mostly negative emotions), decision-making, and memory.

The Spinal Cord

Your spinal cord runs almost the entire length of your back. It transmits information between your brain and your body, and also performs other tasks as well.

The spinal cord meets the brain at the brainstem. From there, 31 pairs of spinal nerves enter the cord.

Along its entire length, your spinal cord links up with peripheral nerves (nerves from the peripheral nervous system) running in from the joints, muscles, and the skin.

Motor signals from the brain move from the spine to the muscles, while efferent signals (sensory information) travels from sensory tissues (like the skin) up to the spinal cord and finally into the brain.

There are circuits within the spinal cord that control reflexive responses, for instance, the involuntary movement made by the arm if it touches a sharp object or a flame of fire.

The circuits in the spine are equally capable of generating complex movements like walking. It is worth noting that the spinal nerves are capable of coordinating the muscles required for walking even without input from the brain.

Let us use an example – if a cat's brain were to be separated from its spine so that there is absolutely no contact between the brain and the cat's body, it will begin walking automatically when placed on a treadmill. The brain is involved only in starting and stopping the process, and making changes, for example, if there is an object in your path.

White and Gray Matter

The central nervous system may be roughly divided into white and gray matter. As a rule of thumb, the outer part of the brain (the cortex) consists of gray matter while the inner area contains white matter.

Both the outer cortex and the inner area contain glial cells (supporting cells) which support and protect the neurons. White matter consists of oligodendrocytes and axons. On the other hand, the gray matter consists of neurons.

Common disorders that affect the central nervous system include:

Trauma: The symptoms of trauma vary, depending on where the injury is located, symptoms range from paralysis to mood disorders.

Infections: The central nervous system is prone to invasion by viruses and micro-organisms such as fungi (cryptococcal meningitis), protozoa (malaria), bacteria (leprosy), or viruses.

Degeneration: Sometimes, the brain or the spinal cord may degenerate. An example is the case in Parkinson's disease. Parkinson's disease is characterized by a gradual degeneration or neurons that produce dopamine. These neurons are located in the basal ganglia.

Structural defects: The major structural defects include anencephaly where some parts of the brain, scalp, and the skull are missing at birth.

Tumors: Tumors (cancerous and noncancerous) affects some parts of the central nervous system. These tumors cause extensive damage and a wide range of symptoms depending on where they develop.

Autoimmune disorders: In some instances, healthy cells in the body may be attacked by the body's own immune system. For example, in acute disseminated encephalitis, the myelin sheath (which insulates the nerves) is attacked, thus, destroying the white matter.

Stroke: Basically, a stroke is a break in blood supply to the brain. This results in lack of oxygen to the brain and subsequent death of the affected tissues.

PERIPHERAL NERVOUS SYSTEM

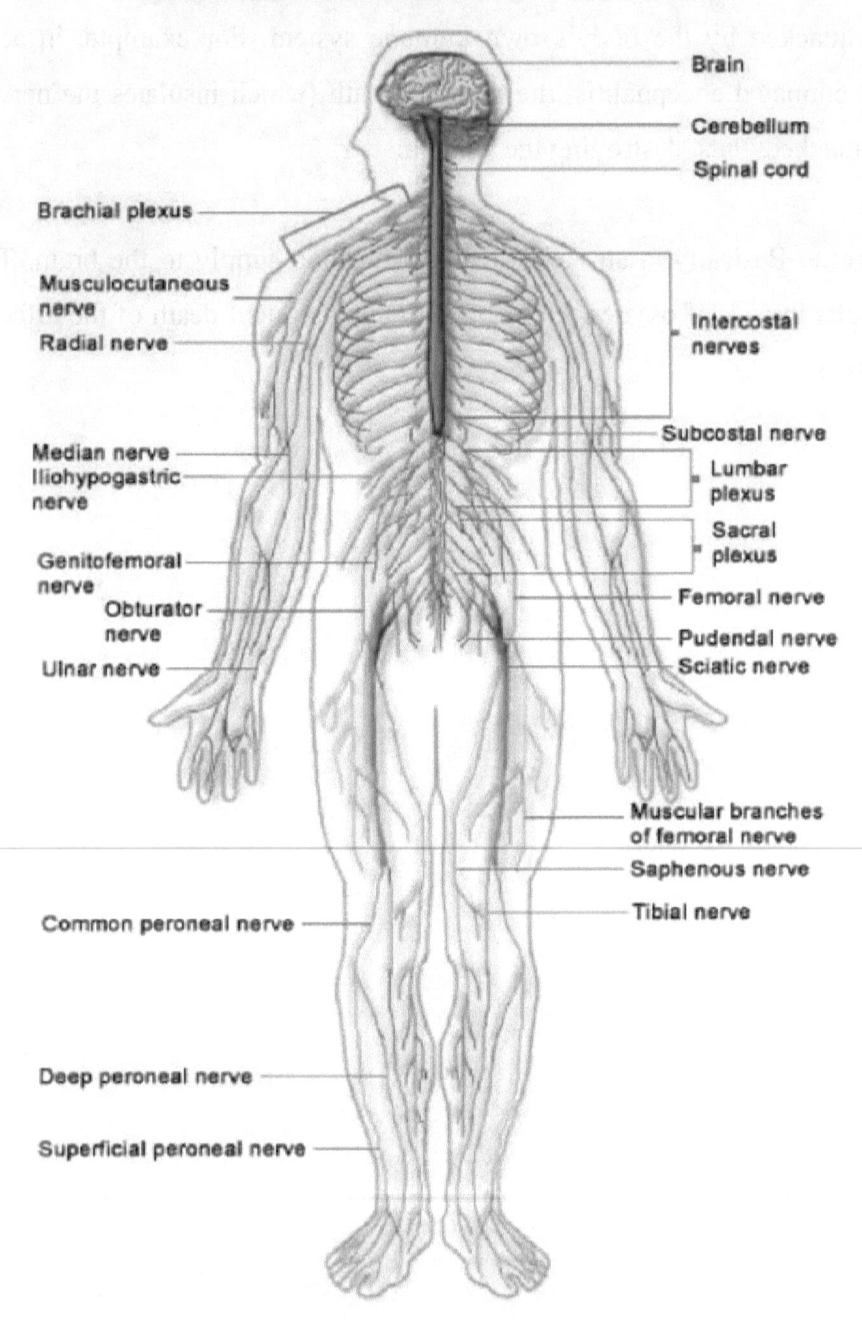

Photo Credit: Socratic QA

The peripheral nervous system is divided into two subsystems – the somatic nervous system & the autonomic nervous system. Both systems contain afferent (sensory) and efferent (motor) components.

The afferent component of the peripheral nervous system consists of afferent neurons or sensory neurons originating from receptors for stimuli to the central nervous system. With the help of receptors, the afferent nerves are able to detect stimuli from the external environment. Such stimuli include hearing, sight, temperature, pressure, etc. Afferent nerves are present in both the somatic and the autonomic nervous systems. The activity of both can be altered with sensory signals.

The efferent component of the peripheral nervous system consists of efferent or motor neurons running from the central nervous system to the effector organ. Effector organs include muscles and glands.

The efferent nerves of the somatic nervous system (of the peripheral nervous system) take charge of voluntary, conscious control of the skeletal muscles (effector organs) through the use of efferent nerves.

Efferent nerves take charge of the visceral functions of the body. These functions include digestion, regulation of heart rate, salivation, urination, etc. the efferent component of this system is further subdivided into sympathetic and parasympathetic motor.

In some cases, the enteric nervous system may be classified as a distinct component of the autonomic nervous system. Some authorities consider it a third independent component of the peripheral nervous system.

Sympathetic and Parasympathetic Nervous System

Both are sub-divisions of the autonomic nervous system. The sympathetic nervous system takes charge of fight or flight responses of the human body. "Fight or flight" indicates the body's response to emergency situations. The sympathetic nervous system originates from the thoracolumbar segments of the spinal cord.

It is equipped with short preganglionic neurons and long postganglionic neurons.

Acetylcholine serves as the main neurotransmitter for the preganglionic nerves while noradrenaline is used by the postganglionic nerves.

CHAPTER 2

ANATOMY & PHYSIOLOGY OF THE CRANIAL NERVES

Your cranial nerves are those nerves that serve as a link between your brain and different parts of your body (head, neck, and trunk). The human body has 12 cranial nerves, each named for their structure or function.

Each cranial nerve has a corresponding Roman numeral between I and XII. This depends on their location from front to back. For instance, the olfactory nerve is the closest nerve to the front of your head, and so it is designated as CN-I.

Functionally, the cranial nerves are classified as sensory or motor. Sensory nerves deal with the senses, like hearing, touch, and smell. Motor nerves on the other hand are concerned with the control of the movement and function of glands or muscles.

This chapter discusses each of the 12 cranial nerves in your body. Keep reading to learn more.

Olfactory Nerve (CN-I)

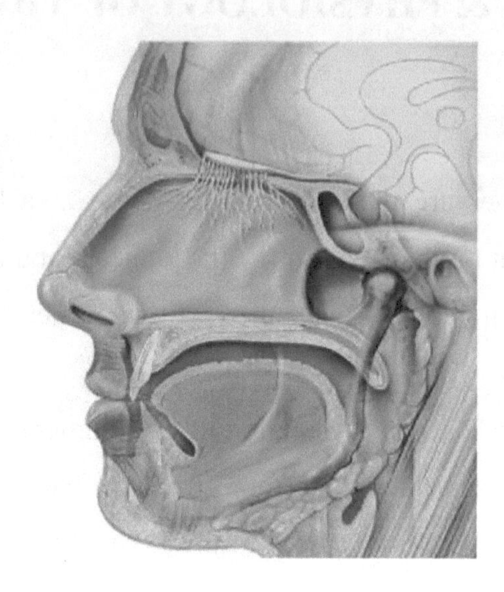

Also known as **CN-I, the olfactory nerve** is the first of 12 cranial nerves located within the head. It relays sensory data to the brain, and it is responsible for the sense of smell.

The receptors of the olfactory nerves are located inside the mucosa of the nasal cavity. Compared to the other nerves, the olfactory nerve does not have two trunks. Instead, its sensory fibers move through cribriform plate of the ethmoid bone – the cribriform plate is a part of the skull that lies behind your nose. Anytime airborne particles and chemicals enter your nose, they hit and interact with these receptors.

Although it is a part of the nervous system, the cranial nerve does not link to the brainstem. The same applies to the optic nerve.

The olfactory nerve is the shortest nerve within the head. It may be affected by lesions caused by trauma, which may in turn be a result of complications of frontal brain lobe tumors, meningitis, etc. this leads to complete or partial absence of the sense of smell. But then, even if your olfactory nerve is damaged, nasal pain will still move through the trigeminal nerve.

In a nutshell, your olfactory nerve transmits sensory smell signals to your brain.

Anytime you inhale molecules with aroma, these molecules will dissolve in a moist surface at the roof of your nasal cavity. This surface is known as the olfactory epithelium. This causes a stimulation of the receptors that generate nerve signals which then move to your olfactory bulb. The olfactory nerve has an oval shape. It contains special nerve cells. From the bulb, the nerves then move into the olfactory tract, which, we have established, lies below the frontal lobe of your brain. The signals are then transmitted to the part of your brain that processes memory and also recognizes smells.

Optic Nerve (CN-II)

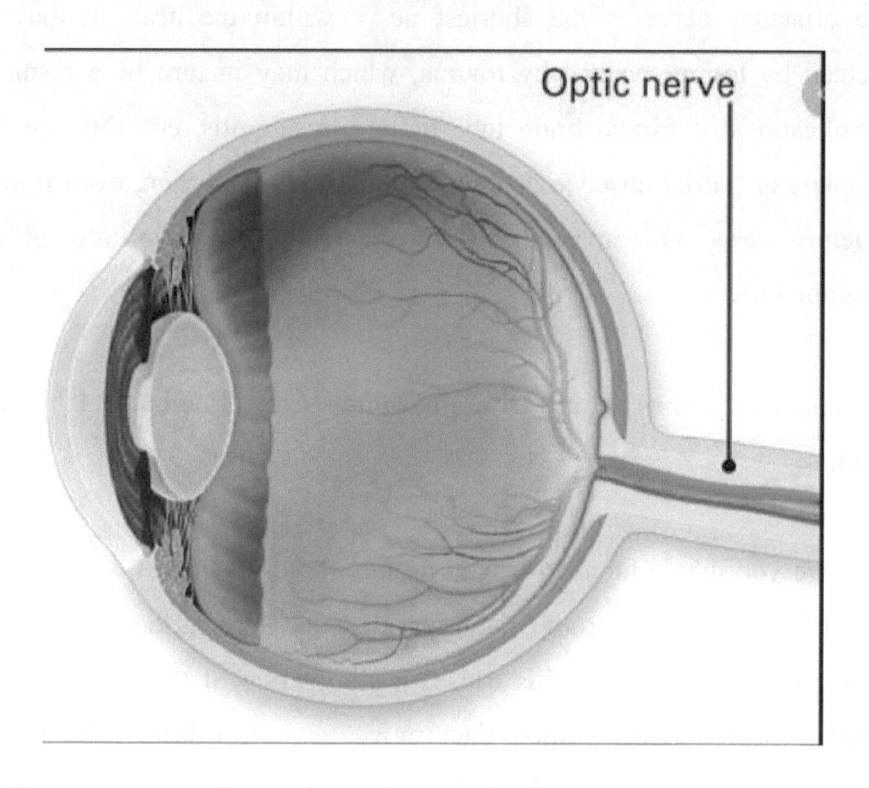

Photo Credit: American Academy of Ophthalmology

The optic nerve is a "vision" nerve. It is a sensory nerve that transmits vision

When light signals get into your eyes, it hits a special group of receptors on your retina. These receptors are called rods and cones. There are many rods on your retina, all having a very high sensitivity to light. The rods are specialized for night or black and white vision.

Unlike the rods, the cones are not many. Also, their sensitivity to light is lower than that of the rods. And then, they are more involved with color vision.

The rods and cones transmit the information that it receives from your retina into the optic nerve. Once the optic nerve gets into the skull, they unite to form a structure known as the "optic chiasm." At the chiasm, nerves from half of each retina give rise to two different optic tracts.

Moving through the optic tracts, the nerve impulses arrive at the visual cortex. The visual signals are then processed by this cortex. The visual cortex lies at the back of the brain.

Oculomotor Nerve (CN-III)

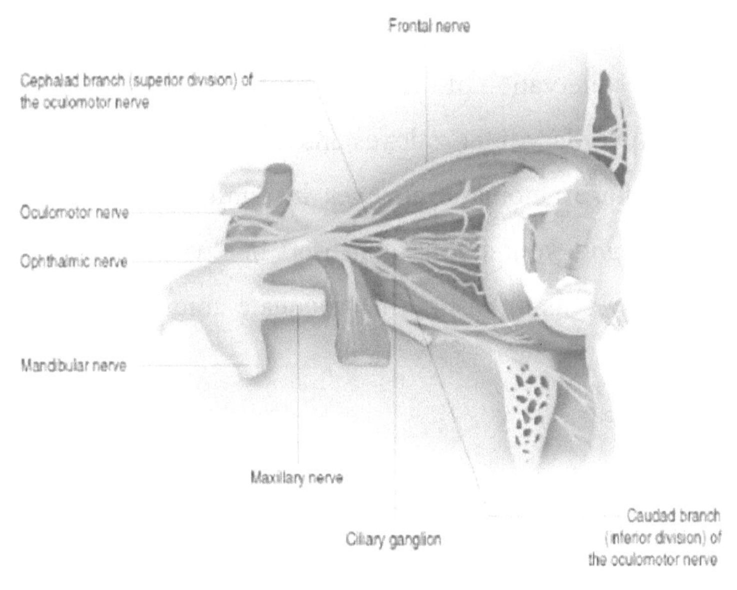

Photo Credit: Science Direct

The oculomotor nerve is the third cranial nerve in the human body. It is responsible for movement of the eyeball and eyelid. It comes after the olfactory and optic nerve.

The oculomotor nerve has two distinct components; each component has its distinct function.

The nerve is responsible for the motor function of four out of the six muscles around your eyes (extraocular muscles). It controls the muscles responsible for the eye's fixation and visual tracking. By visual tracking, we mean the ability of your eye to follow an object in its path as it courses through the field of vision. Fixation means the ability of the eye to focus on an object in its stationary state.

The oculomotor nerve also has a visceral component. The visceral motor component of the oculomotor nerve is responsible for regulation of parasympathetic innervation of the constrictor papillae and ciliary muscles, thus helping in pupillary light reflexes and accommodation. Pupillary light reflexes mean those automatic changes in pupillary dilation. When you look at bright light, your pupils constrict, but when you are in a dark environment, it widens to ensure that adequate amount of light enters the eyes.

Trochlear Nerve (CN-IV)

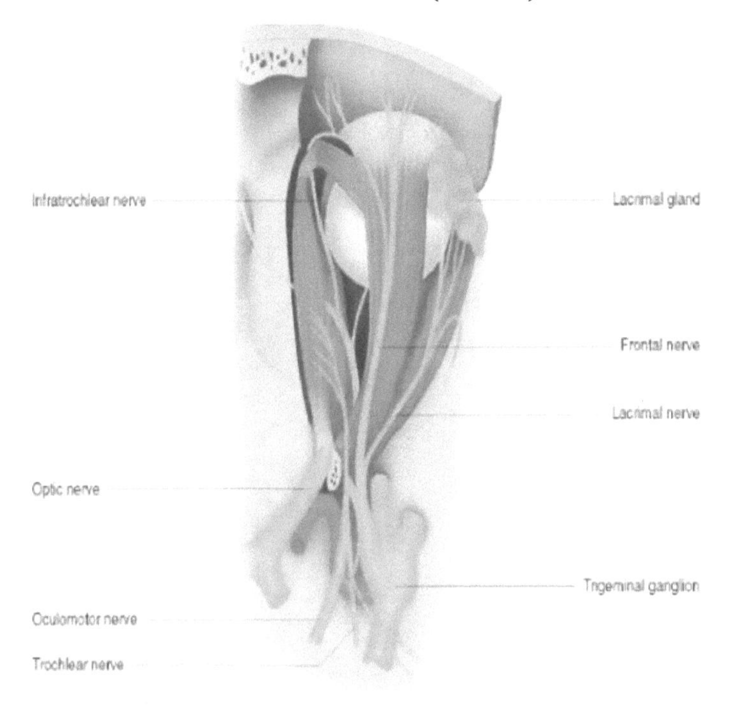

Photo Credit: Science Direct

Your trochlear nerve controls the superior oblique muscle. The superior oblique muscle controls eye movement (inward, outward, and downward).

The trochlear nerve emerges from the back of the brain and continues forward till it meets with the eye sockets. From there, it stimulates the superior oblique muscle.

Trigeminal Nerve (CN-V)

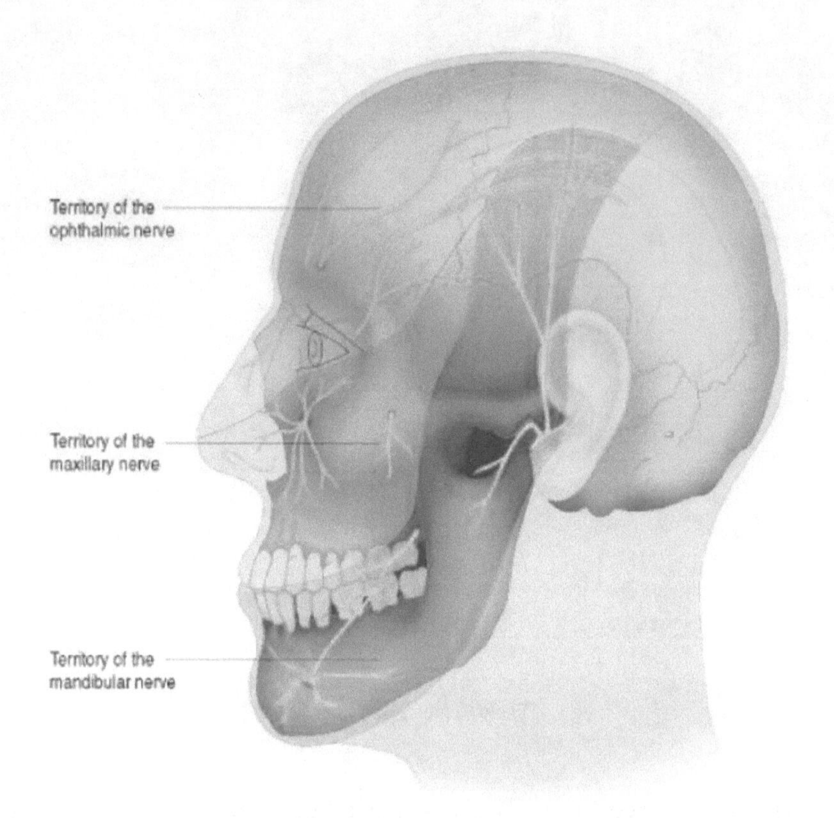

Photo Credit: Science Direct

Your trigeminal nerve is your largest cranial nerve. It has sensory and motor functions.

There are three divisions of the trigeminal nerve. These include:

Ophthalmic (V1): The ophthalmic subdivision of the trigeminal nerve transmits afferent information from upper portion of the face, including the upper eyelids, forehead, and the scalp.

Maxillary (V2): The maxillary subdivision transmits sensory information from the middle portion of the face, including your upper lip, nasal cavity, and cheeks.

Mandibular (V3): It possesses both motor and sensory functions. Sensory information transmitted by the mandibular comes from the lower lip, chin, and ears. It also regulates muscular movements within your ears and jaw.

The origin of the trigeminal nerve is a group of nuclei – a group of nerve cells in the medulla and midbrain regions of your brainstem. These nuclei eventually form a distinct sensory root and motor root.

The trigeminal nerve's sensory root branches into the maxillary, ophthalmic, and mandibular divisions. Conversely, the motor root of the trigeminal nerve passes under the sensory root and is distributed only to the mandibular division.

Abducens Nerve (CN-VI)

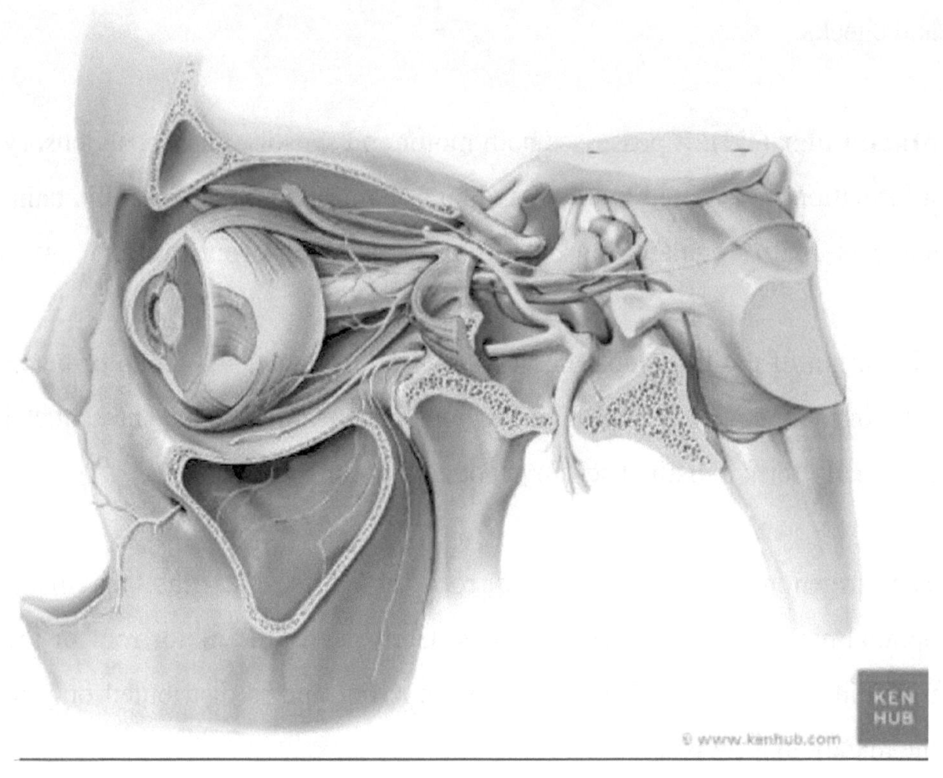

Photo Credit: Kenhub

Abducens nerve controls the muscle associated with movement of the eye. This muscle is called the lateral rectus muscle. The muscle takes charge of outward eye movement. For instance, you could use it to look at the side.

The abducens nerve, begins in the region of the pons in your brainstem. Eventually, it moves into the eye socket, where it regulates the movement of the lateral rectus muscle.

Facial Nerve (CN-VII)

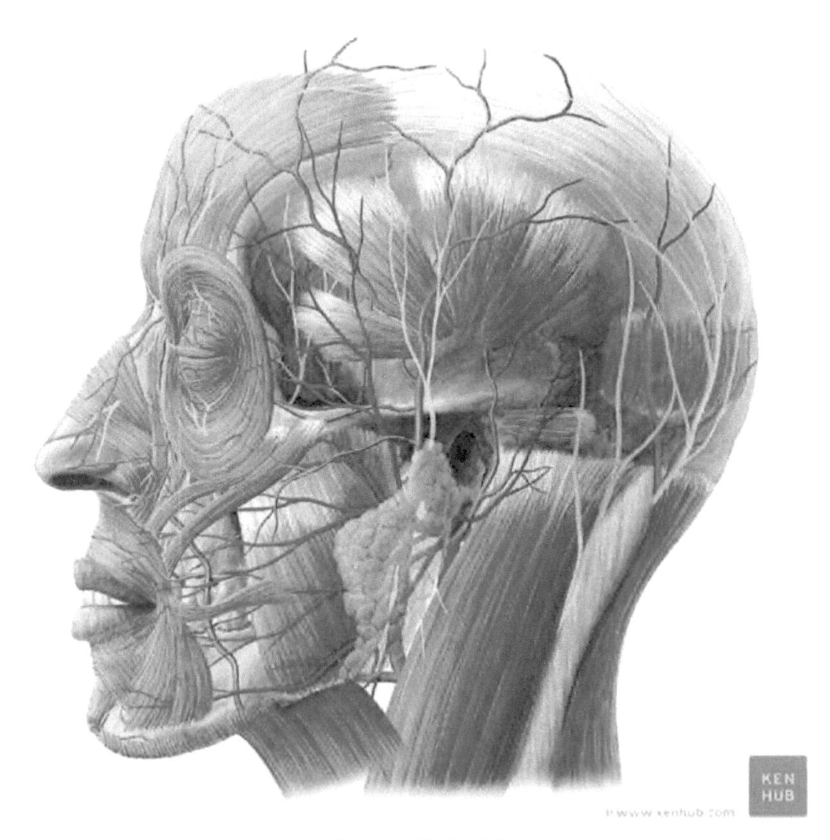

Photo Credit: Kenhub

The facial nerve has both sensory and motor functions. These include:

- Movement of muscles for facial expressions as well as jaw muscles.
- Provides a sensation of taste for a greater portion of your tongue.
- Innervating the glands in your neck and head area, like the lacrimal glands (that produces tears) and the salivary glands.
- Transmits sensory signals from the outer parts of the ear.

The path of your facial nerve is very complex. It starts off in the pons region, containing both sensory and motor roots. Eventually, both nerves fuse to form the facial nerve.

The facial nerve splits into small nerve fibers that stimulates the glands and muscles or provide sensory signals.

Vestibulocochlear Nerve (CN-VIII)

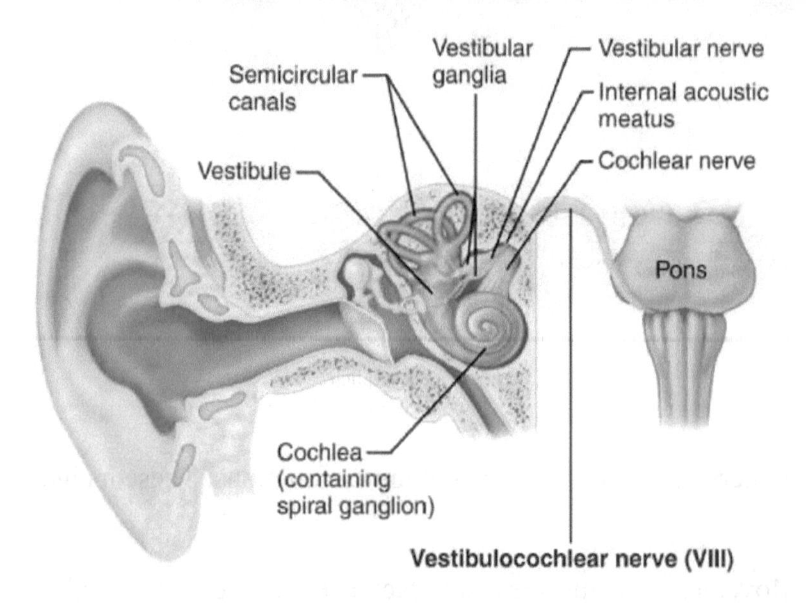

The vestibulocochlear nerve controls sensory functions that involve balance and hearing. It has two divisions – the cochlear division and the vestibular division:

Cochlear division: Special cells within the ear have a high sensitivity to sound vibrations based off the loudness and pitch of the sound. This produces nerve impulses that get transmitted to the cochlear nerve.

Vestibular portion: This is another group of specialized cells with the ability to track the rotational and linear movements of the head. These signals are transmitted to the vestibular nerve and it is involved in equilibrium and balance.

The cochlear and vestibular subdivisions of the vestibulocochlear nerve have distinct origins.

The cochlear originates in the inferior cerebellar peduncle of the brain. The vestibular region, on the other hand, starts off the in the pons and medulla. They both combine to form the vestibulocochlear nerve.

Glossopharyngeal Nerve (CN-IX)

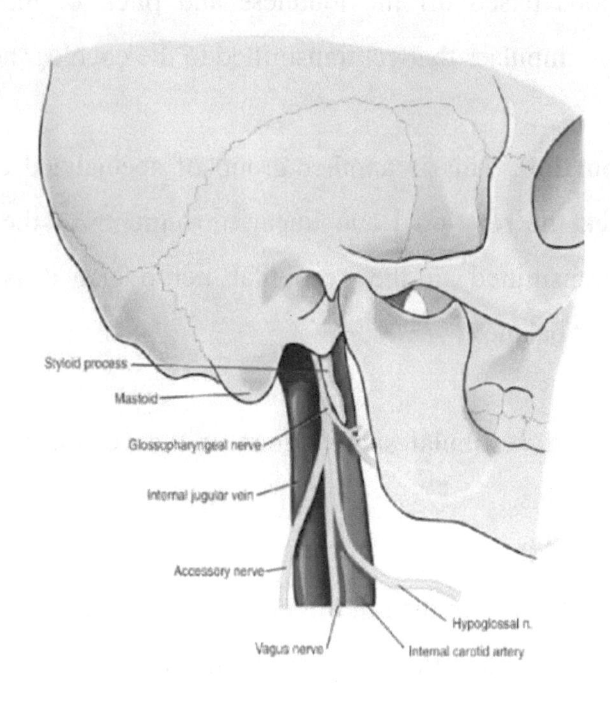

Photo Credit: Science Direct

The glossopharyngeal nerve possesses both sensory and motor functions, such as:

- Transmission of sensory signals from the back of your throat, your sinuses, some parts of your inner ear, and the back of your tongue.
- Provides a sensation of taste for the back of the tongue.
- Stimulates voluntary movements of the stylopharyngeus, a muscle in the back portion of the throat.

The origin of the glossopharyngeal nerve is the medulla oblongata. Eventually, it extends onto the throat and neck region.

Vagus Nerve (CN-X)

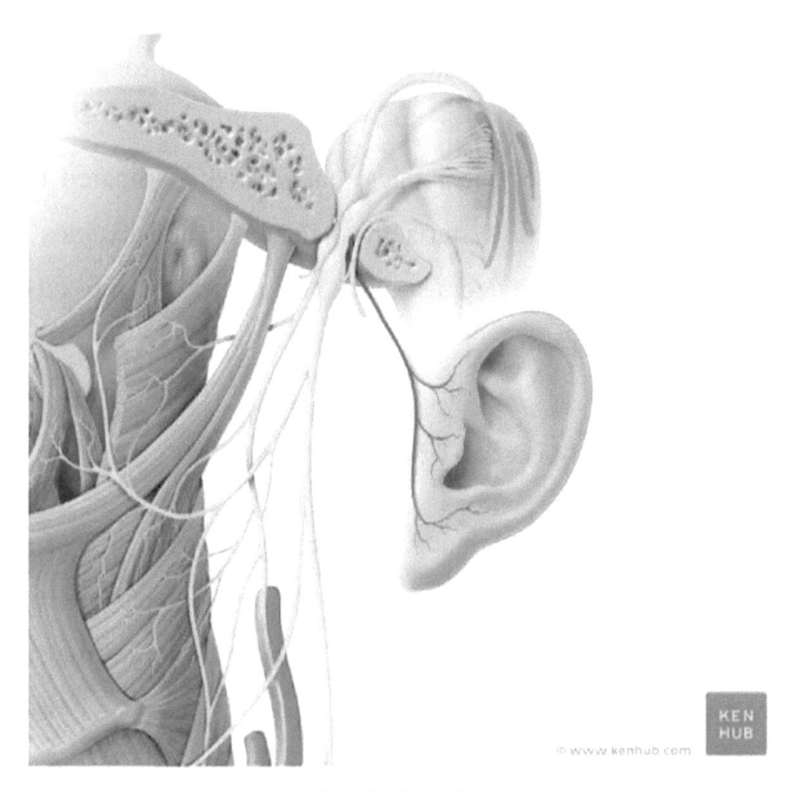

Photo Credit: Kenhub

The Vagus nerve is quite diverse. Like other nerves, it has both sensory and motor functions. These include:

- Transmission of sensory information from the ear canal and parts of the throat.
- Transmitting sensory information from organs in the trunk and chest, like the intestines and the heart for instance.
- Enhances motor control of the throat muscles.

- Stimulates muscles of organs in the trunk and chest, including the muscles that allow movement of food through the digestive system (a process known as peristalsis).
- Provides a sensation of taste near the root of your tongue.

The Vagus nerve possesses the longest pathway of compared to all the cranial nerves in the body. It starts from the head and extends into the abdomen. Specifically, the Vagus nerve originates in the medulla, a component of the brainstem.

Accessory Nerve (CN-XI)

The accessory nerve is a motor nerve that regulates activities of the neck muscles (specifically the Trapezius and Sternocelidomastoid muscles). These neck muscles allow rotation, flexion, and extension of the shoulders and the muscles.

The accessory nerve is subdivided into the spinal and the cranial portions. The spinal portion starts off in the upper region of the spinal cervical cord. On the other hand, the cranial portion starts in the medulla oblongata.

There is a brief meeting of these parts before the spinal portion of the nerve proceeds to supply the neck muscles while the cranial portion follows the Vagus nerve.

Hypoglossal Nerve (CN-XII)

It is the 12th and the last cranial nerve in the body. It is involved in movement of the tongue's muscles. It starts off in the medulla oblongata and then moves into the jaw, where it meets with the tongue.

CHAPTER 3

PHYSIOLOGICAL FUNCTIONS OF THE VAGUS NERVE

The Vagus nerve is known to be the longest cranial nerve that emanates from the brain. Information flowing through the Vagus nerve goes to and from the brain surface to organs and tissues in other parts of the body.

Vagus is derived from the Latin word "wandering." Why is it so named? It is because the Vagus nerve wanders from the brain to organs in the abdomen, chest, and the neck.

The Vagus nerve is the 10th cranial nerve (CN-X).

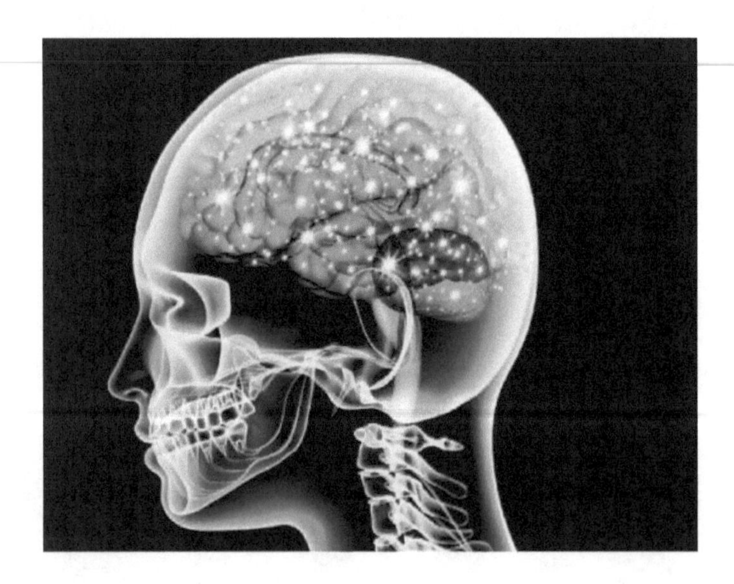

Photo Credit: Medical News Today

The Vagus nerve establishes a connection between the brain and the rest of the body.

There are two bundles of sensory nerve cell bodies in the Vagus nerve, and they link the brainstem to the rest of the body. With the help of the Vagus nerve, your brain can monitor and receive signals about different physiological processes and body functions.

The Vagus nerve provides multiple functions in the nervous system. The same applies to its affiliate parts. Your Vagus nerve is a component of your autonomic nervous system. Of course, you know that your autonomic nervous system consists of sympathetic and parasympathetic parts.

Your Vagus nerve plays vital roles in some of the sensory and motor activities that go on within you.

Essentially, this nerve acts as a circuit, linking the heart, neck, lungs, and the abdomen to the brain.

What is Affected by the Vagus Nerve?

The Vagus nerve serves the body in several ways. The four major functions of the Vagus nerve are:

Sensory function: From the heart, throat, abdomen, and the lungs

Special sensory functions: Enables sensation of taste behind the tongue

Motor function: Takes charge of movement functions for the muscles responsible for speech and swallowing

Parasympathetic: Plays important roles in respiration, heart rate, and digestive tract functioning

The functions of the Vagus nerve can be further sub-divided into seven categories. One of these categories is "nervous system balancing."

We know that there are two subdivisions of the autonomic nervous system: sympathetic and parasympathetic.

The sympathetic side is responsible for creation of alertness, blood pressure, energy, heart rate, and breathing rate.

On the other hand, the parasympathetic side, which is the home of the Vagus nerve, is deeply involved in decreasing alertness, heart rate, and blood pressure. It also helps with digestion, relaxation, and calmness. Because of this, the Vagus also helps with urination, defecation, sexual arousal, and urination.

Other physiological effects of the Vagus nerve include:

Creating a link for brain-gut communication: Your Vagus nerve serves as the pathway through which your brain communicates with your gut and vice versa.

Relaxation with deep breathing: The Vagus nerve is able to send information to the diaphragm. When you breathe deeply, you feel more relaxed.

Decreases inflammation: The Vagus nerve transmits anti-inflammatory signals to every part of the body.

Lowers blood pressure and heart rate: If your Vagus nerve works above the optimal capacity, your heart will be affected. It will be unable to pump enough blood for all parts of the body. Sometimes, over activity of the Vagus nerve can cause organ damage and loss of consciousness.

Fear management: The Vagus nerve transmits information from your gut to your brain. The information transferred is associated with management of fear, stress, and anxiety. This explains the saying "gut feeling." These signals facilitate recovery from scary and stressful situations.

CHAPTER 4

THE ROLE OF THE VAGUS NERVE IN INFLAMMATION

Overview of Inflammation

When an injury swells up, gets reddish in color and hurts, it could be an indication of inflammation. Well, generally speaking, inflammation is a defense mechanism of the human body. It is your immune system responding to an irritant. When you have an inflammation, it means that your body's immune system has recognized a harmful stimulus and has begun the process of healing. This stimulus might be a germ, or a foreign object, maybe a splinter lodged somewhere in your finger.

This means that it is not only when you ooze pus or your wound heals slowly that you have an inflammation. It already starts when your body starts to fight off harmful irritants.
Generally, we have two types of inflammation – acute and chronic.

Acute Inflammation

Tissue damage caused by microbial invasion, trauma, or noxious compounds all contribute to acute inflammation. Acute inflammation has a rapid onset. The severity increases to its peak in a short period while the symptoms may persist for a few days – for instance, as in acute pneumonia or cellulitis. Subacute inflammation is the period between chronic and acute inflammation and lasts between 2 – 6 weeks.

Acute inflammation is characterized by four major features:

Rubor (redness): This is due to vasodilation (increase in the size of the lumen of blood vessels) and increased blood flow.

Calor (heat): Increase in temperature. This increased temperature is localized and also caused by increased blood flow.

Tumor (swelling): This is due to the increased permeability of vessels, allowing loss of fluid into the interstitial space.

Dolor (pain): Pain occurs when the local nerve endings are stimulated. The stimulation may be from chemical or mechanical stimulators.

Phases of Acute Inflammation

There are two stages of acute inflammation – the vascular phase and the cellular phase.

Vascular Phase

The vascular phase is characterized by dilation of small blood vessels adjacent to the injury. When these vessels dilate, there will be an increased flow of blood to the area. The endothelial cells swell initially, and then contract so the space between them can increase. This increases the permeability of the vascular barrier.

The vascular phase of acute inflammation is regulated by chemical mediators. These mediators include:

Histamine
Bradykinin
Complement (C3a, C5a)
Leukotrienes (LTC4, LTD4)
Prostaglandins (PGI2, PGE2, PGD2, PGF2).

When the body is inflamed, the patient will experience exudation of fluid, leading to a net loss of fluid from the vascular space into the interstitial space. The end result is a tumor (edema).

The tissue fluid that forms serves as a medium for the migration of inflammatory proteins (like immunoglobulins and complements). It also helps with the removal of cellular debris and pathogens in the area through lymphatic drainage.

Cellular Phase

Neutrophils are the predominant cells in acute inflammation. Neutrophils are attracted to the site of injury. Chemotaxins causes them to migrate to the site of injury. Chemotaxins are mediators that are released into the blood immediately after a trauma or an injury.

The stages of acute inflammation are vessel vasodilation, exudate formation and neutrophil migration.

There are four stages of neutrophil migration as illustrated in the figure below:

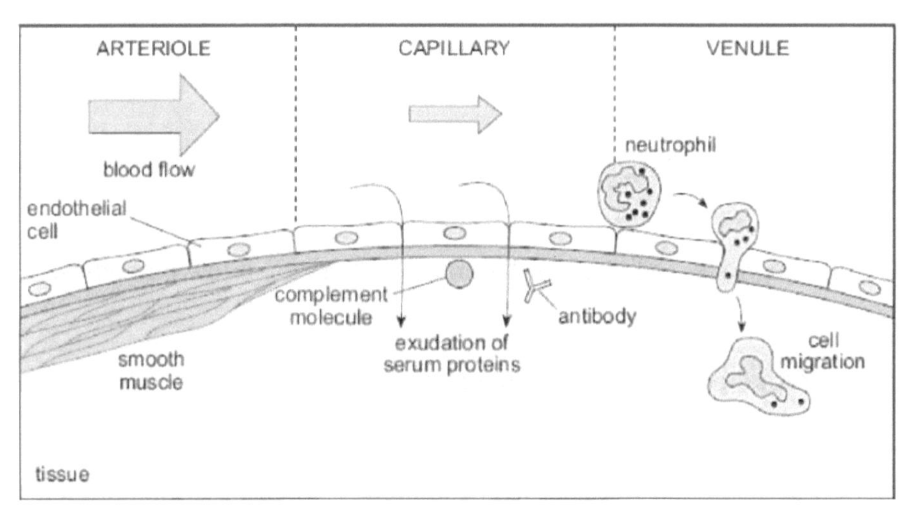

Photo Credit: Teach Me Surgery

Margination – The cells are arranged against the endothelium

Rolling – Neutrophils make close contact with the endothelium and roll along it

Adhesion – The cells are connected to the wall of your endothelium

Emigration – cells move through the vessel wall to the affected area

Once the neutrophils have moved into the region, they identify the foreign body, and this signals the beginning of phagocytosis. During phagocytosis, the pathogen is engulfed and encircled in a phagosome. The phagosome is then destroyed through oxygen-independent and oxygen-dependent mechanisms. A lysozyme is an example of an oxygen-independent mechanism. On the other hand, formation of free radicals is an example of oxygen-dependent mechanism.

Outcome of Acute Inflammation

Following the process of acute inflammation, there are a few outcomes:

Resolution: total destruction and repair of the injury

Formation of scars and fibrosis: happens mostly when the inflammation is significant

Chronic inflammation: occurs from a persisting insult and formation of pus (abscess)

Pus Formation

Pus is a thick fluid that contains dead cells, tissue, and bacteria. It is produced by your body when fighting off an infection, especially bacterial infections.

Pus can assume any color, although this depends on the type of infection, and where the infection is located. The colors of pus include yellow, white, brown, and green. Sometimes, it may be odorless, and at other time, foul-smelling.

What causes pus formation?

Sometimes, we may have an infection that can trigger pus formation. These infections happen when fungi or bacteria gain access to our body, mainly through:

- Poor hygiene
- Broken skin
- Inhaled droplets from a sneeze or a cough

When your immune system detects an infection, it releases neutrophils to destroy the bacteria or fungi. Some of these neutrophils die off in the process of fighting the infection. And so, the abscess on your skin is an accumulation of these dead cells.

Many kinds of infection can cause pus. Infections more prone to pus include those involving Streptococcus pyogenes or Staphylococcus aureus. These bacteria release toxins that damage the tissues, resulting in the formation of pus.

Where Does Pus Come From?

Generally, pus forms into an abscess. An abscess is a space or cavity created by tissue trauma or tissue breakdown. Abscesses can form inside your body or on the surface of your body. It is important to note that some parts of your body may be more exposed to bacteria than others. This makes them more vulnerable to infections.

Some of these areas include:

The urinary tract. Escherichia coli is responsible for most infections of the urinary tract. E. coli is found mostly in the colon. It is very easy to introduce E. coli into your urinary tract – just wipe from back to front after a bowel movement and it jumps in. The cloudy urine that you pass when you have a UTI, is caused by pus.

The mouth. Our mouths are moist and warm. There is no better environment for bacterial growth. If there is a crack in your tooth or an untreated cavity, then a dental abscess might develop. Oral bacterial infections can cause the collection of pus on your tonsils. This results in a condition known as tonsillitis.

The skin. Abscesses form on the skin due to infection of a hair follicle, or a boil. Severe acne can also cause pus to form. Leaving your wounds open exposes your skin to infections that trigger pus formation.

The eyes. Pus may form after an eye infection, like a pink eye for instance. Other eye problems, like embedded grit or dirt, or a blocked tear duct, can trigger the formation of pus in your eye.

Does Pus Cause Any Symptoms?

If you have any pus-causing infection, then it is likely that you will have other symptoms. If the infection occurs on the surface of your skin, you will notice redness on the skin, usually warm, around the abscess, in addition to red streaks surrounding the abscess. The area might also be swollen and painful.

Internal abscesses usually do not have visible symptoms. However, one might experience some flu-like symptoms, including:

- Chills
- Fever
- Fatigue
- Getting rid of pus

Treatment for pus depends on the severity of the infection causing it. For small abscesses forming on the surface of your skin, you may apply a warm, wet compress to help it drain. Apply the compress few times daily for several minutes.

Never succumb to the urge to squeeze out pus. While you may think that you are getting rid of it, you are only pushing more of it into your skin. Squeezing pus also creates new wounds. And this may cause another infection.

If your pus is bigger, deeper, or harder to reach, call the attention of your doctor. They can draw out the pus with a needle or create a small incision to facilitate drainage of the pus. If it is a large abscess, they may insert a drainage tube or pack it using medicated gauze.

Deeper infections or infections that refuse to heal might require antibiotic therapy.

Chronic Inflammation

Chronic inflammation is a slow, long-term inflammation – one that may last for months or even years on end. There are variations to the extents and effects of chronic inflammation with the case of the injury and the body's ability to repair the damage.

What Cells are involved in chronic inflammation?

The microscopic features of a chronic inflammation are much different from that of an acute inflammation.

Chronic inflammation is generally described in terms of the cells that are present:

Macrophages: Macrophages are present in both acute and chronic inflammation. They play important roles in phagocytosis, synthesis of cytokines, and antigen presentation.

Lymphocytes: Lymphocytes perform immunological functions. We have T and B lymphocytes. B cells give rise to antibodies while T cells have cytotoxic functions.

Plasma cells: Basically, plasma cells are B lymphocytes that produce antibodies. The presence of plasma cells is an indication that the inflammation has been there for quite some time.

Eosinophils: usually found in parasitic infections and allergic reactions.

Myofibroblasts/fibroblasts: They are recruited by macrophages and produce collagen to help with healing and repair.

Generally, chronic inflammation has no specific morphology. However, there may be variations in the proportions of each cell type depending on the condition. For instance, rheumatoid arthritis presents with plasma cells, while lymphocytes are abundant in chronic gastritis.

You see, chronic inflammatory diseases are the primary cause of death in our world. According to the World Health Organization (WHO), chronic diseases constitute the greatest threat to human health. It is believed that the prevalence of diseases linked to chronic inflammation will increase consistently over the next three decades in the United States.

In the year 2000, at least 125 million Americans were living with chronic conditions, and 21 percent of these (61 million) had at least one chronic disease. Rand Corporation estimates that in 2014, nearly 60% of US citizens had at least one chronic condition, while 42 percent had more than one condition, and 12% of adults had no less than 5 chronic conditions.

Globally, most people will die with at least three of the chronic diseases such as heart disorders, stroke, obesity, diabetes, cancer, and chronic respiratory diseases.

Let us examine the prevalence of some diseases whose onset is triggered by chronic inflammation:

Diabetes: In 2015, at least 30.3 million people had diabetes in America. That is a whopping 9.4% of the population according to the American Diabetes Association. What is more? It was the 7th major cause of death in the United States.

Cardiovascular diseases: According to the American Heart Association, at least one in every three deaths is caused by cardiovascular diseases. That is approximately 8,000,000 deaths in the United States. Globally, cardiovascular diseases contribute to 30 percent of all deaths, with most of them due to coronary heart disease, followed by stroke and heart failure.

Arthritis and Joint Diseases: At least 350 million people are affected by arthritis and joint diseases globally. The United States alone accounts for 43 million sufferers. This number is expected to exceed 60 million by 2020. At least 2.1 million Americans suffer from rheumatoid arthritis.

Allergies: Allergies are the sixth major cause of chronic diseases in the United States, and at least 50 million Americans are affected on a yearly basis. At least 24 million Americans are affected by Asthma with more than 6 million being children. In 2015, 8.4% of children and 8.2% of adults were diagnosed with hay fever.

Chronic Obstructive Pulmonary Disease (COPD): COPD was the third major cause of death as at 2014. At least 15.7 million Americans were diagnosed with COPD. Most features of acute inflammation continue even as the inflammation progresses to the chronic stage. These include vasodilation (expansion of blood vessels), increased blood flow, increased permeability of the capillaries, and movement of neutrophils through the walls of the capillary and into the infected tissue. However, the composition of your white blood cell changes soon, with the neutrophils getting replaced by lymphocytes and macrophages. Thus, what could be considered as the hallmarks of chronic inflammation include infiltration of primary inflammatory cells like plasma cells, macrophages, and lymphocytes in the tissue site, release of inflammatory cytokines, enzymes, and growth factors, thus contributing to advancement of tissue damage, and secondary repair including formation of granuloma and fibrosis.

Reducing Inflammation is a Function of the Vagus Nerve

Inflammation is the underlying cause of many chronic diseases. The Vagus nerve plays a very important role in reducing inflammation.

Clinical research has shown that there is a very strong link between stress, inflammation, and the immune system.

Your Vagus nerve (cranial nerve X) is the major nerve in the parasympathetic division of the autonomic nervous system. It is the key communication route between your brain, cardiovascular system, gut, and your immune system. This pathway (which is bidirectional), travels from the brainstem, courses through the chest, into your abdominal region, before branching into multiple organs. Such a wide pathway is it not? Well, this explains why it is called the Vagus, a Latin term for wandering, as we saw in the first part of this chapter.

Your body system has a very intricate connection. As such, it needs something to help coordinate the information that flows through it. This function is performed by your Vagus nerve. Signals are transmitted from your brain to your abdominal organs, chest organs, as well as from the organs and gut back to the central nervous system (the brain). Orchestration of this communication network is handled by the Vagus nerve. It does this by sending signals to the brain to produce hormones and neurotransmitters, coordinating responses, regulating reactions to stress, and checking inflammation.

For instance, the Vagus nerve is involved in the coordination of the parasympathetic relaxation response, aiding the control and slowing down of heart and breathing rate, promoting relaxation, stimulating digestion, and restoring peace and calm within the body. This relaxation response is coordinated by acetylcholine, a neurotransmitter, which appears to be a very important brake in the body's inflammation.

Vagal Tone and its Importance

The Vagus nerve is one of the key control centers for the human body. Its health is of great importance to the health of your immune system, brain, and the general inflammatory state.

Activities in the Vagus nerve tend to be stronger in some people than in others. This explains why some people are able to relax more quickly after stress. Vagal tone is the term that describes the strength of your vagal response.

Low vagal tone is a major contributory factor to chronic inflammation. Studies have shown that people suffering from various inflammatory conditions, like rheumatoid arthritis, usually have low heart rate variability. This low vagal tone enhances the production of pro-inflammatory cytokines, resulting in an increase in activities of the sympathetic nervous system and stress hormones, thus contributing to systemic inflammation.

The Brain – Gut Connection

You have heard of "gut feelings" right? Basically, these are sensations that emanate from your belly, indicating that there is a connection between your gut and your brain.

What is more, recent research has shown that your brain has great influence over your gut health, and your gut in turn can affect the health of your brain.

This communication link between your brain and your gut is referred to as the brain – gut connection, or the gut-brain axis.

Your gut and your brain are connected physically and biochemically in many ways. Let's see how these two systems connect.

The Nervous System and the Vagus Nerve

The central nervous system (made of the brain and the spinal cord) contains a lot of neurons – about 100 billion in the brain alone (1). These neurons instruct your body on how to behave.

The interesting news is that your gut also contains a large number of neurons – around 500 million (2). These gut neurons are connected to your brain via nerve cells in your nervous system.

We have established on many occasions that the Vagus nerve is one of the longest nerves in the nervous system, as well as in your gut. It is bi-directional, meaning that it transmits information in both directions (3, 4).

For instance, in animal studies, it has been shown that stress affects the transmission of signals through your Vagus nerve, and also causes issues with the gastrointestinal tract (5).

Also, a study (6) involving humans found that patients with irritable bowel syndrome or Crohn's disease had a very low Vagal tone, indicating an inhibition of Vagal nerve function.

Another study has found that feeding mice with a probiotic caused a drastic reduction in their blood levels of stress hormone. But then, upon cutting their Vagus nerve, the probiotic had no effect (7).

This indicates that the Vagus nerve is a chief component of the gut-brain axis and is deeply involved in stress.

Neurotransmitters

The brain and the gut are also linked to each other through neurotransmitters. Neurotransmitters are chemical substances produced at the tail end of neurons.

Brain neurotransmitters control emotions and feelings.

For instance, serotonin, a neurotransmitter, contributes to happy feelings and also regulates your circadian rhythm (8).

The interesting point is that most of the neurotransmitters are also produced by cells in your gut as well as the many microbes that live there. Your gut produces most of the serotonin found in your body (9).

There is another neurotransmitter (GABA) produced in the gut. Specifically, it is produced by microbes in the gut. It helps to regulate feelings of anxiety and fear (10).

The microbes in your gut affect inflammation.

There is a connection between the immune system and the gut-brain axis.

Your gut and gut flora have an important role to play in inflammation and also in your immune system by regulating what enters your body and what is excreted by your body (11).

If your immune system is overstretched or overworked, it can trigger inflammation, which is linked to various brain disorders like Alzheimer's disease and depression (12).

Lipopolysaccharide is one of the inflammatory toxins made by some bacteria. It triggers inflammation if an excess of it passes from the digestive system into the blood. This happens when the gut barrier is leaky, thus allowing entry of bacteria and lipopolysaccharide into the blood.

Inflammation and high blood levels of lipopolysaccharide have been associated with dementia, severe depression, and schizophrenia (13).

Vagus Nerve and Better Mental Health: An Interesting Connection

The importance of good mental health cannot be overemphasized. It is a truth that cannot be denied. Taking care of your mental health is just as important as taking care of your physical health. There are many techniques, hacks, and tools to boost your mental wellbeing and sustain it. But how can you do this?

See, you have to stimulate your Vagus nerve to increase its tone. This is the key to ensure better mental health. By stimulating the Vagus nerve, its tone increases and activates the parasympathetic nervous system, thus allowing your body to relax faster after stress.

So, how can you stimulate your Vagus nerve? There are a few tips. We will just list them out here and explain the major ones in detail in "**Chapter 6**: **Activating the Healing Power of the Vagus Nerve**."

Ways to stimulate your Vagus nerve:

- Cold exposure
- Slow and deep breathing
- Exercising
- Meditation and yoga-like stretching/poses
- Laughing, socializing, and having gratitude
- Probiotics

CHAPTER 5

STRESS AND THE NERVOUS SYSTEM

The Basics of Stress

Stress is a situation that triggers a specific biological response. Anytime you come face-to-face with a major challenge, or a particular situation, your body experiences a hormonal and chemical surge.

Stress sets in motion your body's fight-or-flight response, enabling you to fight the stressor or run away from it. Under normal circumstances, your body should relax after fighting the stressor. Excessive stress can negatively impact your long-term health.

Stress is not necessarily a bad thing.

Our hunter-gatherer ancestors used stress as a survival instinct. It is important in the modern world. Stress becomes a healthy feature when it helps us to avoid an accident, meet a deadline, or maintains your wits and sanity in the midst of chaos.

Every human being feels stressed at times, but our experiences differ. What you find stressful may be different from what another person does. Public speaking is a good example. While some are thrilled by the very thought of mounting the podium, others become paralyzed by the very idea.

We have agreed that stress is not necessarily a bad thing. For instance, you will be stressed on your wedding day, but you would not consider that a bad form of stress would you?

However, consistent stress is not healthy. Stress should be temporary. Once you have crossed the fight-or-flight moment, your breathing rate and your heart rate should decrease, and your muscles should relax. It is expected that your body will return to its natural state of rest without any negative effects.

On the other hand, consistent stress may have deleterious effects on your mental and physical health.

Chronic stress is a common occurrence. It is worth noting that at least 80% of Americans experience at least one symptom of stress in a month. Up to 20% experience chronic stress.

Life is what it is, and so, it is practically unrealistic to completely eliminate stress from our lives. But we can try to avoid it when possible and manage it when it is unavoidable.

Stress Hormones

When you are in the face of danger, your hypothalamus reacts. Your hypothalamus is located at the base of your brain. It sends hormone and nerve signals to your adrenal glands. Upon receiving the signals, your adrenal glands release a lot of hormones. These hormones prepare your body to face danger while also raising your chances of survival. Adrenaline is a prominent example. It is also known as epinephrine. Adrenaline works rapidly. It:

- Increases the heartbeat
- Increases your rate of breathing
- Eases glucoses utilization by your muscles
- Facilitates contraction of deep blood vessels so that more blood is directed to the muscles
- Stimulates respiration
- Inhibits the production of insulin

All these are helpful at the moment. However, frequent surges of adrenaline can lead to:

- Damage of blood vessels
- Hypertension or high blood pressure
- Stroke or an increased risk of heart attack
- Headaches
- Insomnia
- Anxiety
- Weight gain

As important as adrenaline is, it is not the primary stress hormone. The primary position is reserved for cortisol.

As the primary stress hormone, cortisol plays a vital role in stressful conditions. Functions of cortisol include:

- Increasing blood glucose concentration
- Facilitating effective utilization of glucose by the brain
- Increasing the accessibility of substances that enhances tissue repair
- Placing a restraint on nonessential body functions when the body is faced with a life-threatening situation
- Altering the response from the immune system
- Dampens the growth process and functioning of the reproductive system
- Influences those parts of the brain that control motivation, fear, and mood.

These functions equip you to deal with stress effectively. It is normal, and very essential for human survival. But if your cortisol remains consistently at high levels, it impacts your health negatively. It leads to:

- High blood pressure
- Weight gain
- Insomnia
- Osteoporosis

- Type 2 diabetes
- Fatigue and lethargy
- Brain fog (mental cloudiness) and problems with memory
- A weak immune system, leaving you at risk of infections

It also affects your mood negatively.

Types of Stress

There are three major types of stress namely:

- Acute stress
- Episodic acute stress
- Chronic stress

Acute Stress

Everyone experiences acute stress. It is the immediate reaction of the body to a new and challenging situation. Example of acute stress is what you feel when you have had a narrow escape from a car accident.

You may also experience acute stress from something that you enjoy doing. An example would be the somewhat-scary yet equally thrilling experience that you get when you are on a roller coaster or when skiing.

Such incidents do not cause any harm to the body. Heck! Your body might even benefit from them. Stress trains your body and your brain to respond in the best possible way to future stressful situations.

Once you have overcome the danger, your body system returns to normal. But severe acute stress is a different ball game entirely. Severe acute stress can result in post-traumatic stress disorder and other mental defects.

Episodic Acute Stress

This is when acute stress occurs frequently in episodes. It may happen to people that are often anxious or worried about things they fear may happen. Your life may seem chaotic and you seemingly jump from one crisis to the next.
Some professions also put an individual at high risk of frequent stress. Such include firefighters and law enforcement agents. Just like severe acute stress, episodic acute stress also has negative effects on your mental and physical wellbeing.

Chronic Stress

A person has chronic stress when he or she experiences high levels of stress for a long period. Prolong stress has negative impacts on a person's health. It may contribute to:

- Cardiovascular disease

- Anxiety
- Depression
- High blood pressure
- A weak immune system

Chronic stress also causes ailments such as an upset stomach, headache, and difficulties with sleep.

Stress and the Nervous System

Frequent and chronic stress affects our bodies negatively. We hear this every time, but what are the implications of stress on our nervous system?

We have discussed extensively on the two subdivisions of the autonomic nervous system – the sympathetic and the parasympathetic nervous system.

The parasympathetic nervous system plays a very important role in body homeostasis – it maintains equilibrium in our body physiology.

Our sympathetic nervous system was initially used to prepare our bodies for an imminent threat, like getting chased by bears and tigers.

However, these things do not happen anymore. So rather, we use it to stress over trivial issues. For instance, like someone speaking ill of your dress or fashion style.

When our sympathetic nervous system is switched on, our heart rate speeds up. This is followed by dilation of the bronchial tubes in our lungs, contraction of muscles, drastic reduction in the production of saliva, inhibition of several digestive functions, and conversion of glycogen to glucose.

This explains why overuse of the sympathetic nervous system could be associated with weight gain, heart disease, asthma, and other health problems.

Many times, we have no control over daily stressors, but we can always change our response to these stressors.

Effects of Stress on the Brain

The brain is a major component of the central nervous system, and like other parts of the body, is also affected by stress. Let us see how this happens.

Chronic stress is a major risk factor of mental illness: A study documented in the journal Molecular Psychiatry (14) has shown that chronic stress causes long term changes in the brain. This, perhaps, explains why people who suffer frequent chronic stress are also more prone to anxiety and mood disorders later in life.

University of California researchers performed a number of experiments examining the impact of chronic stress on the brain. Results from these studies showed that chronic stress caused the creation of fewer than normal neurons.

When this happens, some parts of the brain will have an excess of myelin, which interferes with the balance and timing of communication. It was also discovered that stress can affect the hippocampus negatively.

It changes the structure of the brain: The same study conducted by University of California researchers showed that chronic stress causes prolong alterations in the brain's structure and function.

The brain consists of support cells and neurons, called "gray matter." The gray matter plays essential roles in problem-solving, decision-making and other high-order cerebral functions. The brain also has what is known as "white matter." White matter consists of all the axons that link with other regions of the brain to facilitate seamless flow of information. White matter derives its name from the fatty sheath called myelin. The fatty myelin is white in color. It surrounds the axons and facilitates speedy transmission of electrical signals used for information flow throughout the brain.

Excessive production of myelin caused by chronic stress, causes lasting changes in the structure of the brain. It also distorts the balance between gray and white matter.

Stress kills the brain cells: Researchers from the Rosalind Franklin University of Medicine and Science discovered that just one socially-stressful event could destroy new neurons in the hippocampus of the brain (15).

Your hippocampus is a part of your brain that plays very important roles in emotion, memory and learning. It is also one of the sites for neurogenesis (or formation of brain cells). In the experiment conducted by this research team, young rats were placed in a cage with two older rats for just 20 minutes. The young rats were then bullied or subjected to the aggressiveness of the older rats. Upon examining the young rats, it was discovered that their cortisol levels had risen to six times higher than that of rats which had not been exposed to such events.

Upon further examination, it was found that although the stressed and non-stressed rats had developed the same number of neurons, the number of neurons in the stressed rats was markedly reduced just a week later.

Stress shrinks the brain: Even in healthy people, chronic stress can cause shrinkage of those areas of the brain associated with metabolism, memory, and emotions.

Researchers have found that most mental disorders may be attributed to excessively high levels of stress. In a particular study, Yale University researchers examined 100 healthy participants who gave useful information about the stressful times they've experienced. The researchers discovered that exposure to stress resulted in small gray matter in the prefrontal cortex. The prefrontal cortex is that region of the brain associated with emotions and self-control (16).

Frequent, chronic stress on its own may not have much impact on the brain volume, but it may increase your vulnerability to brain shrinkage especially when you are battling with traumatic stressors.

It hurts your memory: Have you ever tried recalling the details of a stressful event? You will agree that it was somewhat difficult to remember. Even minor stress can affect your memory. You may find it hard to remember where you dropped your car keys, or where you left your cell phone when you are running late for work.

According to a 2012 research (17), the spatial memory is usually affected by stress. Spatial memory may be described as the ability to recall the position of objects in the environment.

The overall impact of stress hinges on several variables. Timing is one of these. Studies have shown that stress which comes immediately after learning can help with memory consolidation.

Conversely, stress also impedes memory. For instance, research has shown that exposure to stress immediately after a memory retention test leads to reduced performance in both animals and humans.

From chronic stress to inflammation: The pathway to ill health.

What determines your future health are not your genes, but by the choices you make every day.

If you have followed us from the very first page of this book, then we are sure you have understood the basics of stress. It is a complex process, but the fact remains that chronic stress ultimately leads to chronic inflammation. You may be wondering, how exactly does chronic stress lead to chronic inflammation, after all, cortisol is anti-inflammatory? Well, that is a good question and we are happy you have asked it.

You see, we all experience stress at some point in our lives – whether at work, at school, or even while doing chores at home. Let's use the work place as an example.

No matter the kind of job you have, it is certain that you will face minor hassles each day. It could be traffic jams, long and boring commutes, angry clients, breakdowns of your computer system, sensory overload, or very tight deadlines.

In some cases, you will not even notice that chronic stress has become a major part of you because you have adapted to it. Feeling distracted, tired, or bugged by the nagging sense that you are running out of time becomes a normal thing to you.

You disregard the fact that life is moving so fast and accept that it normal to be pressured at work. You consider it is a sacrifice you should make if you must get ahead in your career.

Unfortunately, there is nothing right about living in a state of overdrive, and it harms your body more than you may realize. Chronic stress, and its sister, inflammation, are major underlying factors in most diseases and illnesses.

Stress and inflammation are triggers of obesity, cardiovascular disease, type 2 diabetes, autoimmune disorders, asthma, Alzheimer's, arthritis, and cancers. What makes stress and inflammation more dangerous is the fact that they can take years, sometimes decades, before the first symptoms of associated disease manifests.

Evolution has not equipped humans to live a constant state of stress. Rather, our fight-and-flight instincts have evolved to help us survive immediate and temporary threats, such as an electric shock, or an attack by a wild animal.

When something triggers your stress response, your blood pressure and heart rate shoots, and your immunity gets suppressed. Digestion is suppressed, temporarily though, while your breathing gets faster. These reactions all occur instantly so your body is always prepared to flee from the pending threat as fast as you can.

We are sure a lot of people reading this may not face daily threats to their bodily existence, but then, many live in a constant state of fight-or-flight, subjecting themselves to chronic stress as they live through daily hassles.

Once the stress mechanism has been activated, there is not much you can do to override it because the relevant hormones (adrenalin and cortisol) readily latch onto their receptors on the membrane of cells, triggering a series of events within the cells.

For instance, in the bone marrow, chronic stress can turn your immune system into promoters of inflammation, a process that starts with genetic changes. If you are exposed to some stressors everyday of your life, then there is a big chance that you will develop chronic inflammation which will ultimately result in chronic illnesses.

You see, chronic inflammation differs from acute inflammation. In acute inflammation, there are symptoms, many symptoms such as redness or swelling etc. Conversely, in chronic inflammation, there are very few symptoms, if any.

Because symptoms are always expressed in acute inflammation, it has taken clinicians decades to identify chronic inflammation as a major (and invisible) culprit in many chronic illnesses globally.

Research on the exact biochemical links between chronic inflammation and stress is ongoing. However, we know that both factors contribute massively to compromising the immune system and the development of so-called "lifestyle disorders." Lifestyle disorders are illnesses that develop due to our daily lifestyle. How we live each day has the ability to influence the expression of disease-related gene mutations, including genes for heart disease, Alzheimer's disease, diabetes, and cancer.

Summarily, your future health is predetermined not by your genes, but by your daily choices. That is why it is important to live healthy, and healthy living includes a "near stress-free life."

CHAPTER 6

ACTIVATING THE HEALING POWERS OF THE VAGUS NERVE

Many people are yet to understand that the Vagus nerve is probably the most important nerve in the human body.

Compared to other nerves, what happens in this Vagus doesn't stay there. The Vagus nerve links the brain stem to lungs, heart, and the gut. It also innervates the liver, the gallbladder, spleen, female reproductive organs, ureter, kidneys, tongue, ears, and the neck.

It powers our parasympathetic nervous system (this we know), and controls visceral (unconscious) functions of the body from maintenance of heart rate to sweating, digestive functions, and breathing.

It also helps with the regulation of blood pressure and blood glucose balance, promotion of general kidney function, release of testosterone and bile, stimulation of saliva secretion, control of taste functions and release of tears. It is also deeply involved in female orgasms and fertility issues in women.

We also know that the Vagus nerve has fibers that innervate every internal organ in the body. The vagal nerve connection between the heart, gut, and the brain plays a very vital role in managing and processing our emotions.

This explains the strong “gut feeling” that we have towards intense emotional and mental states.

Dysfunction of the Vagus nerve can trigger a wide range of problems, such as bradycardia (slow heart rate), obesity, difficulty swallowing, fainting, gastrointestinal disorders, deficiency of vitamin B12, mood disorders, seizures, impaired cough, and chronic inflammation.

On the other hand, stimulation of the Vagus nerve improves the following conditions:

- Heart disease
- Anxiety disorder
- Tinnitus
- Alcohol addiction
- Obesity
- Migraines
- Leaky gut
- Alzheimer’s
- Poor blood circulation
- Cancer
- Mood disorders

Acetylcholine is the major neurotransmitter of the Vagus nerve. It stimulates muscle contractions in the parasympathetic nervous system. A neurotransmitter facilitates transmission of signals from point to point. It is released at the end of a nerve fiber. For instance, if our brain fails to communicate with our diaphragm through the release of acetylcholine from the Vagus nerve, then breathing would cease automatically.

Certain substances like mercury and Botox can interfere with the production of acetylcholine. Clinical research and experience has shown that Botox does have the potential to shut down nerve functions, which results in death.

Mercury impedes smooth functioning of acetylcholine. When mercury attaches to the protein thiol in the receptors of your heart muscle, it prevents the heart muscle from receiving the Vagus nerve electrical impulse for contraction. What follows, will be cardiovascular problems.

The 3000 tons of mercury that fills our atmosphere can interfere with production of acetylcholine.

The Vagus nerve may also be damaged by alcoholism, diabetes, infections of the upper respiratory organs by viruses, or accidental severing of part of the Vagus nerve during surgery.

Stress may also cause inflammation of the nerve. Same goes for anxiety and fatigue. Even a bad posture can impact negatively on the Vagus.

Diet is also believed to contribute to Vagus nerve health. Junk foods that are high in carbs and fats reduce the sensitivity of the Vagus nerve. Heavily spiced foods can also cause the nerve to misfire.

The Vagus nerve has great healing powers, most of which can be unlocked by improving the vagal tone. The vagal tone can be improved naturally via stimulation with techniques that can be performed at home. Strengthening your vagal tone will help with mood, digestion, and general wellbeing.

The following techniques can help to rekindle the healing powers of your Vagus nerve.

The Deep-Breathing Technique

We will call it box breathing, or maybe square breathing. This technique is used for slow, deep breaths. It can boost concentration and performance while also acting as a potent stress reliever. Box breathing is also known as four-square breathing.

Anyone can benefit from the deep-breathing technique, especially those that are interested in stress relief or meditation.

The deep-breathing technique may be particularly useful for people with a lung disease such as chronic obstructive pulmonary disease.

Getting Started

Before you begin, ensure that you sit upright in a comfortable chair. Your feet should be rested flat on the floor. Make sure your environment is quiet and stress-free so you can focus on your breathing.

Relax your hands on your lap with your palms facing up, and then focus on your posture. You should sit in a straight-up posture. With this, you will be able to breathe deeply.

When you are set, start with the following steps:

Exhale slowly: Sitting in an upright posture, exhale slowly through your mouth, making sure that all the oxygen gets out through your mouth. Maintain your focus and be conscious of what you are doing.

Inhale slowly: Breathe in slowly and deeply through your nose. Count to four while breathing in. Feel the air as it fills up your lungs, a particular section at a time, until the lungs are completely filled and the air flows into your abdomen.

Hold your breath: Do this to the count of four.

Exhale once again: Exhale slowly through your mouth to the count of four, flushing out all the air from your abdomen and lungs. Ensure you have a conscious feel as the air leaves your lungs.

Hold your breath again to the slow count of four before repeating the process.

How does the box breathing technique help?

According to a study by the Mayo Clinic (18), there is enough evidence to prove that purposeful deep breathing can calm and regulate functions of the autonomic nervous system.

The autonomic nervous system regulates temperature and other involuntary body functions. It can reduce blood pressure while also providing a sense of calm.

During the moment that you hold your breath, CO2 builds up in your blood. Increase in blood concentration of carbon (IV) oxide boosts the cardio-inhibitory response of the Vagus nerve during exhalation, and then stimulates the parasympathetic system. This allows you to feel calm and relaxed in your body and mind.

Deep breathing reduces stress and serves as a “mood improver.” Hence, it is an exceptional treatment for panic disorder, generalized anxiety disorder, post-traumatic stress disorder, and depression.

It also helps with the treatment of insomnia by calming your nervous system at night just before you fall sleep. It is equally helpful with pain management.

Loving Kindness Meditation

The loving kindness meditation, also known as Metta meditation trains your heart to be loving, kind, humble and forgiving, while also opening your heart to rewire old habits of responding to others. Loving kindness meditation also increases your vagal tone.

Instructions for Loving Kindness Meditation:

- Sit in a quiet place, free of any form of distraction or interruptions. Sit comfortably, in a straight and relaxed position.
- Place your palms gently on your thighs and close your eyes.
- As you meditate, say these phrases in your mind. Never rush. And be gentle if your mind starts wandering away. Simply repeat the phrases over and over for as long as you like but it shouldn't be less than four times.

First, direct the meditation towards yourself. It is difficult we agree, but you can do it.

"I will be happy."
"I will be safe."

"I will live a life free from pain."
"I will live with ease."

Channel your focus towards someone that is close to you, a loved one, maybe someone from your past or present, who still keeps in touch, or has passed away, friend, family, spiritual mentor etc.

Just imagine that the person is seated right in front of you.

Now direct the loving kindness towards them:

"You will be happy."
"You will be safe."
"You will live a life free from pain."
"You will leave with ease."

After meditating for a few rounds, focus your attention on someone neutral and then offer them meditation.

MOST IMPORTANT, and for **YOUR BENEFIT, also extend the practice to a person you are having difficult times with. **

You can then extend the practice to include those living in your neighborhood, in your city, and the world at large.

"May everyone live happy."

"May everyone be safe."
"May everyone be free from pain."
"May everyone live a life of ease."

Consistent practice of loving kindness meditation daily for six weeks has been proven to improve overall health, wellbeing, and vagal tone.

Yoga-like Stretching and Poses

Disclaimer: An alternative to the practice of yoga would be embracing stretching techniques. Stretching classes can be found online or could be offered in your local community recreation centers.

Studies have demonstrated a link between yoga and increased vagal tone, as well as general improvement in the parasympathetic activity (19, 20).
A study involving 12 weeks of yoga intervention showed improvements in anxiety and mood compared to walking exercises. According to the study, yoga increases thalamic levels of GABA which are associated with decreased anxiety and improved mood (19).

Yoga also supports overall physical and mental health (21, 22). Yoga practice increases flexibility of both the physical body and the nervous system. Studies have shown that yoga has tremendous benefits including improved vagal tone, recovery from trauma, and stress reduction.

With this, you can become skilled at switching between parasympathetic and sympathetic nervous systems with ease and at your own will. The following yoga techniques will boost your development of a healthy vagal tone, relaxation and energizing, and as maintenance of balance in your life.

Conscious breathing:

Breathing is a quick way to alter the balance between your sympathetic and parasympathetic nervous system. Vagus nerve yoga focuses on diaphragmatic breathing as well as extension of the duration of exhalation.

With this, it counterbalances overstimulation of the sympathetic nervous system. Studies have shown that slow, diaphragmatic breathing improves the vagal tone and maintains it at healthy levels (23).

Ujjayi pranayama plays a very important role in conscious breathing. It is a form of yogic breathing that allows slight constriction at the back of your throat through engagement of your whisper muscles.

Here's how you can learn the Ujjayi pranayama:

- Exhale out of your mouth.
- Breathe in, and exhale again, but this time through your nose.

You will notice that the breath sounds louder, often like the ocean waves. Start an even count as you inhale and exhale. For deeper relaxation, increase the length of your exhalation as compared to inhalation. For instance, you may count to four while inhaling and count to 6 or 8 while exhaling. This helps to calm your parasympathetic nervous system.

Half smile:

A half smile is a great way to influence your mental state and buildup a peaceful and serene feeling. Because the Vagus nerve innervates the muscles of your face, you can increase vagal tone by allowing your facial muscles to relax and then turning your lips slightly.

Doing this engages what Dr. Stephen Porges calls the "social nervous system." When smiling, imagine your jaw relaxing, and a calm feeling running through your face, your head as a whole, and extending down to your shoulders. Also observe the subtle changes in your emotions and thoughts.

Open up your heart:

The Vagus nerve can be stimulated gently using yoga postures that open across your throat and your chest. Sit with your hands on your shoulders. Inhale while expanding across the front of your chest, opening your elbows wide, and lifting your chin.

Exhale, while you tuck your chin and contract your elbows in front of your heart. Breathe deeply several times while meditating. More focus should be placed on inhalation. It is uplifting and stimulating. Allow your inner self to expand into your open heart.

Wake and stretch:

If you are finding it difficult to wake in the morning or if you feel sluggish and tired in the afternoons, then yoga can give your mind and body a gentle but stimulating touch. You can stand in postures such as the warrior (virabhadrasana) to wake your body and invigorate your mind.

Observe as your feet connect to the earth to stay grounded so you can get energized in a balanced manner. Allow your breath to flow in a rhythm so you can be rooted and connected to your body's sensations.

Release your belly:

You can tone the Vagus nerve as it passes through your belly. Assume a table position with your knees underneath your hips and your hands underneath your shoulders. If you feel some form of discomfort on your knees, you can fold a blanket and place it underneath.

While inhaling, raise your head gradually while lowering your hips and your belly as you switch to the cow pose. While exhaling, lower your hips and your head and then lift your spine into the cat pose. Time yourself appropriately with your breath. Repeat as many times as possible creating a gentle massage for your spine and belly.

Yoga Nidra:

Yoga Nidra or restorative yoga calms your nervous system. An instance is the "yogic sleep" or what we would call meditation-in-relaxation. It is the antidote to our modern and extremely stressful lifestyle. It creates an opportunity to restore your body and mind through accessing your parasympathetic nervous system.

To do the Yoga Nidra, lie on the floor in a relaxing position. Be conscious of your body and breath. Create a channel, or outlet for your feelings, including any sensation of heaviness, constriction, or tension.

Remain still for up to 30 minutes for a relaxing and nourishing experience.

Massage

Massaging some key areas like the carotid sinus (on your neck) helps to stimulate your Vagus nerve. Studies have shown that it can reduce seizures (24). Please note, massaging the carotid sinus on your own is not recommended as it can cause fainting or other risks.

One may also activate the Vagus nerve through a pressure massage. A pressure massage boosts weight gain in infants by stimulating the gut, an action that is believed to be mediated by Vagus nerve activation (25, 26).

Reflexology foot massages also improves vagal activity as well as heart rate variability while reducing blood pressure and heart rate (27).

Cold Water Exposure

A 2008 study 28 involving 10 healthy subjects shows that when the human body adjusts to cold temperatures, the sympathetic nervous system experiences a decline, while activities of the parasympathetic system are stimulated – an action believed to be mediated by the Vagus nerve. In the present study, cold temperature was pegged at 50°F (10°C).

Animal studies have shown that sudden exposure to cold (39°F/4°C) increases activation of Vagus nerve in rats (29).

Although not many studies have been done on the effect of cold water splash on the Vagus nerve, many are proponents of this traditional cooling method.

But come to think of it. We all took cold showers before heating systems were invented. Anecdotally, cold tubs are widely used in Japan, while many Northern nations do ocean dips for special occasions during the early spring or winter.

It takes some time for one to get fully used to cold showers though. Some people believe that it is good to dip one's face in cold water before starting a cold shower.

Also, it is important that you consult your doctor before doing a cold-water splash. Cold showers might not be good for people with heart disease, or those who have a high risk of it.

Why? Because sudden exposure to the cold can constrict the blood vessels, which in turn increases heart rate and blood pressure.

Tai Chi

Slow deep breathing and the intent to relax are major components of the Qi Gong and Tai Chi practice. Tai chi activates the parasympathetic nervous system, resulting in the lowering of the acidity in the internal environment. A combination of the soft spiraling and the stretching movements of Qi Gong and Tai chi, together with deep breathing, increases oxygen demand.

This further activates the alkaline response, aiding internal healing and tissue regeneration.

20 minutes of Qigong and Tai Chi helps to activate the body's relaxation response. You will have a calm, more centered, relaxed, and alert feeling. Your body returns to a neutral state for improved longevity, happiness, and health.

Sun Exposure

It is possible that exposure to the sun may stimulate the Vagus nerve.

Studies have shown that Alpha-MSH protects rodents from damage due to a stroke.

Prevention occurs by activating the Vagus nerve, which impedes the inflammation process (30, 31).

When alpha-MSH is injected into the brain, it causes moderate excitation of the Vagus nerve in some conditions (32).

Exposure to the sun boosts alpha-MSH synthesis. However, saying that sun exposure can stimulate the Vagus nerve might be a long stretch (33).

Fasting

Reducing calories, as well as fasting intermittently causes an increase in heart rate variability, a factor believed to be a marker of vagal tone (34).

Intermittent fasting is believed to improve heart rate variability. However, this claim has not been verified by any clinical trials.

According to a particular theory, the Vagus nerve might initiate a reduction in metabolism during fasting. According to the theory, the Vagus

can detect a shortfall in blood glucose level and a decrease in chemical and mechanical stimuli from the gut. This increases vagal impulses from the liver to the brain, which tones down the metabolic rate (35).
Results from animal studies indicate that hormones like NPY increases while CRH and CCK decreases during fasting (35).

The reverse may be the case after eating. Satiety signals from the gut appear to boost sympathetic activity and stress responsiveness (high CRH, CCK, and low NPY) (35).

The Vagus nerve also increases the sensitivity of animals to estrogen during hunger states. A study conducted on female rodents shows that fasting increases the number of estrogen receptors in certain regions of the brain (PVN and NTS), which may be mediated by the Vagus (36).

Closing Remarks

We truly hope that the information in this book has been useful to you, and that it may add value to your daily journey of using the healing power within you, by harnessing the innate power of your Vagus nerve.

Like many things in life and health, the true secret lies in learning how to look "within" and practicing the "within", as the "without" (or outside of one's self) requires a dependency on outside sources and is limited by the availability of the outside and your ability to pay for the outside "help".

REFERENCES

1. Herculano-Houzel S. The human brain in numbers: a linearly scaled-up primate brain. Front Hum Neurosci. 2009; 3:31. Published 2009 Nov 9. doi:10.3389/neuro.09.031.2009
2. Mayer EA. Gut feelings: the emerging biology of gut-brain communication. Nat Rev Neurosci. 2011;12(8):453–466. Published 2011 Jul 13. doi:10.1038/nrn3071
3. Breit S, Kupferberg A, Rogler G, Hasler G. Vagus Nerve as Modulator of the Brain-Gut Axis in Psychiatric and Inflammatory Disorders. Front Psychiatry. 2018; 9:44. Published 2018 Mar 13. doi:10.3389/fpsyt.2018.00044
4. Bonaz B, Bazin T, Pellissier S. The Vagus Nerve at the Interface of the Microbiota-Gut-Brain Axis. Front Neurosci. 2018; 12:49. Published 2018 Feb 7. doi:10.3389/fnins.2018.00049
5. Sahar T, Shalev AY, Porges SW. Vagal modulation of responses to mental challenge in posttraumatic stress disorder. Biol Psychiatry. 2001;49(7):637–643. doi:10.1016/s0006-3223(00)01045-3
6. Pellissier S, Dantzer C, Mondillon L, et al. Relationship between vagal tone, cortisol, TNF-alpha, epinephrine and negative effects in Crohn's disease and irritable bowel syndrome. PLoS One. 2014;9(9): e105328. Published 2014 Sep 10. doi: 10.1371/journal.pone.0105328
7. Bravo JA, Forsythe P, Chew MV, et al. Ingestion of Lactobacillus strain regulates emotional behavior and central GABA receptor

expression in a mouse via the Vagus nerve. Proc Natl AcadSci U S A. 2011;108(38):16050– 16055. doi:10.1073/pnas.1102999108

8. Anguelova M, Benkelfat C, Turecki G. A systematic review of association studies investigating genes coding for serotonin receptors and the serotonin transporter: I. Affective disorders. Mol Psychiatry. 2003;8(6):574–591. doi:10.1038/sj.mp.4001328
9. Yano JM, Yu K, Donaldson GP, et al. Indigenous bacteria from the gut microbiota regulate host serotonin biosynthesis [published correction appears in Cell. 2015 Sep 24;163:258]. Cell. 2015;161(2):264–276. doi: 10.1016/j.cell.2015.02.047
10. Mazzoli R, Pessione E. The Neuro-endocrinological Role of Microbial Glutamate and GABA Signaling. Front Microbiol. 2016; 7:1934. Published 2016 Nov 30. doi:10.3389/fmicb.2016.01934
11. Rooks MG, Garrett WS. Gut microbiota, metabolites and host immunity. Nat Rev Immunol. 2016;16(6):341–352. doi:10.1038/nri.2016.42
12. Lucas SM, Rothwell NJ, Gibson RM. The role of inflammation in CNS injury and disease. Br J Pharmacol. 2006;147 Suppl 1(Suppl 1): S232–S240. doi: 10.1038/sj.bjp.0706400
13. Kelly JR, Kennedy PJ, Cryan JF, Dinan TG, Clarke G, Hyland NP. Breaking down the barriers: the gut microbiome, intestinal permeability and stress-related psychiatric disorders. Front Cell Neurosci. 2015; 9:392. Published 2015 Oct 14. doi:10.3389/fncel.2015.00392

14. Chetty, S., et al. (2014).Stress and Glucocorticoids Promote Oligodendrogenesis in the Adult Hippocampus. MOLECULAR PSYCHIATRY, 19, 1275-1283. doi: 10.1038/mp.2013.190.
15. Society for Neuroscience. (2007, March 15). The day after a stressful event, rats lose brain cells. SCIENCEDAILY.
16. Hathaway, B. (2012, Jan. 9). Even in the healthy, stress causes brain to shrink, Yale study shows. YALENEWS.
17. Ansell, E. B., Rando, K., Tuit, K., Guarnaccia, J., & Sinha, R. (2012).Cumulative Adversity and Smaller Gray Matter Volume in Medial Prefrontal, Anterior Cingulate, and Insula Regions. BIOLOGICAL PSYCHIATRY, 72(1), 57-64. doi: 10.1016/j.biopsych.2011.11.022.
18. Mayo Clinic. (2020). Decrease stress by using your breath. [online] Available at: https://www.mayoclinic.org/healthy-lifestyle/stress-management/in-depth/decrease-stress-by-using-your-breath/art-20267197?pg=2 [Accessed 24 Feb. 2020].
19. Streeter CC, Whitfield TH, Owen L, et al. Effects of yoga versus walking on mood, anxiety, and brain GABA levels: a randomized controlled MRS study. J Altern Complement Med. 2010;16(11):1145–1152. doi:10.1089/acm.2010.0007
20. Brown RP, Gerbarg PL. SudarshanKriya yogic breathing in the treatment of stress, anxiety, and depression: part I-neurophysiologic model [published correction appears in J Altern Complement Med. 2005 Apr;11(2):383-4]. J Altern Complement Med. 2005;11(1):189–201. doi:10.1089/acm.2005.11.189

21. Hayes M, Chase S. Prescribing yoga. Prim Care. 2010;37(1):31–47. doi: 10.1016/j.pop.2009.09.009
22. Akhtar P, Yardi S, Akhtar M. Effects of yoga on functional capacity and well-being. Int J Yoga. 2013;6(1):76–79. doi:10.4103/0973-6131.105952
23. Lehrer, P. and Gevirtz, R. (2014). Heart rate variability biofeedback: how and why does it work? Frontiers in Psychology, 5.
24. Laine Green A, Weaver DF. Vagal stimulation by manual carotid sinus massage to acutely suppress seizures. J ClinNeurosci. 2014;21(1):179–180. doi: 10.1016/j.jocn.2013.03.017
25. Field T, Diego M, Hernandez-Reif M. Potential underlying mechanisms for greater weight gain in massaged preterm infants. Infant Behav Dev. 2011;34(3):383–389. doi: 10.1016/j.infbeh.2010.12.001
26. Field T, Diego M, Hernandez-Reif M. Preterm infant massage therapy research: a review. Infant Behav Dev. 2010;33(2):115–124. doi: 10.1016/j.infbeh.2009.12.004
27. Lu WA, Chen GY, Kuo CD. Foot reflexology can increase vagal modulation, decrease sympathetic modulation, and lower blood pressure in healthy subjects and patients with coronary artery disease. AlternTher Health Med. 2011;17(4):8–14.
28. Mäkinen TM, Mäntysaari M, Pääkkönen T, et al. Autonomic nervous function during whole-body cold exposure before and after cold acclimation. Aviat Space Environ Med. 2008;79(9):875–882. doi:10.3357/asem.2235.2008

29. Yuan PQ, Taché Y, Miampamba M, Yang H. Acute cold exposure induces vagally mediated Fos expression in gastric myenteric neurons in conscious rats. Am J PhysiolGastrointest Liver Physiol. 2001;281(2): G560–G568. doi:10.1152/ajpgi.2001.281.2. G560
30. Ottani A, Giuliani D, Mioni C, et al. Vagus nerve mediates the protective effects of melanocortins against cerebral and systemic damage after ischemic stroke. J Cereb Blood Flow Metab. 2009;29(3):512–523. doi:10.1038/jcbfm.2008.140
31. Ottani A, Giuliani D, Galantucci M, et al. Melanocortins counteract inflammatory and apoptotic responses to prolonged myocardial ischemia/reperfusion through a Vagus nerve-mediated mechanism. Eur J Pharmacol. 2010;637(13):124–130. doi: 10.1016/j.ejphar.2010.03.052
32. Richardson J, Cruz MT, Majumdar U, et al. Melanocortin signaling in the brainstem influences vagal outflow to the stomach. J Neurosci. 2013;33(33):13286–13299. doi:10.1523/JNEUROSCI.0780-13.2013
33. Hiramoto, K., Yamate, Y., Kobayashi, H. et al. Long-termultraviolet A irradiation of the eye induces photoaging of the skin in mice. Arch Dermatol Res 304, 39–45 (2012).https://doi.org/10.1007/s00403-011-1183-3
34. Mager DE, Wan R, Brown M, et al. Caloric restriction and intermittent fasting alter spectral measures of heart rate and blood pressure variability in rats. FASEB J. 2006;20(6):631– 637. doi: 10.1096/fj.05-5263com

35. Székely M. The Vagus nerve in thermoregulation and energy metabolism. AutonNeurosci. 2000;85(1-3):26–38. doi:10.1016/S1566-0702(00)00217-4

36. Estacio MA, Tsukamura H, Yamada S, Tsukahara S, Hirunagi K, Maeda K. Vagus nerve mediates the increase in estrogen receptors in the hypothalamic paraventricular nucleus and nucleus of the solitary tract during fasting in ovariectomized rats. Neurosci Lett. 1996;208(1):25–28. doi:10.1016/0304-3940(96)12534-9

Made in United States
Troutdale, OR
12/02/2023